Life Drawing

Life Drawing

Poems by

Kris Spencer

Cover design by Shay Culligan
Cover photograph by Todd Antony

ISBN: 978-1-63980-243-2

Kelsay Books
502 South 1040 East, A-119
American Fork, Utah 84003
Kelsaybooks.com

For Julie, who draws to us all that is good in life

Acknowledgments

Some of the poems in *Life Drawing* were previously printed in the following journals:

Acumen: "Wrestling Cholitas," "The Song of the Self," "Funeral Song"

Allegro: "Golden Girl"

Balloons Literary Journal: "Imagine," "We Need to Find a Forest"

Black Fox Literary Magazine: "Rotator Cuff," "Of the Styles of Handwriting and the Direction of the Lines Written"

Briefly Write: "Magpies," "The Piano Tuner"

Capsule Stories: "White Light," "Life Drawing"

Drawn to the Light: "Ode to Yellow"

Fenland Poetry Journal: "Man Walks into a Bar," "Enough," "Ode to White"

Hyacinth Review: "Ode to the Light on the Sea at High Tide," "Ode to Looking into the Shadows on Market Day"

Literary Bohemian: "Tinnitus," "How to Make a Scarecrow"

MORIA Literary Magazine: "On Sending Ted Kooser Unquiet Landscape"

Orchards Poetry Journal: "L-O-V-E," "The Surface Holds"

Selcouth Station: "Ode to Jean-Michel Basquiat in Which Certain Things Are Crossed Out"

The Storms: "The Enormous Matter of Landscape"

There is advice out there for poets to set aside what they have written for a while, better to see it for what it is. I have tried this in my writing, but I am impatient. Happily, I have had support and advice from other poets. Crucially, early in my writing, Rachel Long spoke to me with all the grace, intelligence, and care which is there in her own work. With John Glenday, I have felt as if guided around bogs and gullies to some wind-blown fell, persuaded to throw off all that is vain or extravagant to help the climb. Julia Webb has shown me how poems work with and against each other. I have tried to learn from each a sense of balance and rightness. Thanks to all who have helped me. My mistakes remain my own.

Contents

Part 3

Part 1

A book,
a book full
of human touches,
of shirts,
a book
without loneliness.

—Pablo Neruda, *Odes to Common Things*

Ode to Yellow

The yellow of toast.
Linguine with lemon butter sauce
eaten in the sunshine
is four times yellow.
Minion yellow. Pikachu yellow.
Simpsons yellow.
The pale yellow of insect blood.
The girl in the saffron dress
walking home from church
crosses over from the shade
to avoid the boys from the estate.
A yellow leaf on a cold day.
The halos of marigolds
and the sun when we saw
the pollen come up.
Sulfurous lemon-yellow
of the evening sky.
Indian Yellow, made
from the urine of cows.
Orpiment. Tartrazine.
Eye-saver yellow.
Snake venom yellow.
Van Gogh with mouth full
of Chrome Yellow,
toxic as battery acid.
Vermeer Yellow. Turner Yellow.
Mondrian Yellow.
Winifred Nicholson Yellow.
Olafur Eliasson at Tate Modern:
monofrequency light
emits yellow that reduces
the viewers' spectral range.

In a meadow's haze, yellow
is a buttercup held to my chin.
As he climbs into bed with us
my son says, *today is a yellow lamp.*

White Light

In the simplicity of the great white light all color lives
—Winifred Nicholson

Winifred Nicholson would collect
wildflowers and place them in a jug
for a lamp on a dull day. To a buttery mass

of blossoms she once added two violet
everlasting peas and saw the yellows
break free like music. We throw

the shutters back. Air rushes in
with the flinty smell of rain, and rasp
of insects and shifting grass. Breaking

into luminosity: my hands at work,
your shoulder moving as you wake,
the roundness of our baby's heel. Outside,

a maple turns from brown to green
with the passing of a cloud. And, as the light
goes, the flowers glow on the table.

The Surface Holds

*Reality lies not in the appearance of the subject but in the extent to which
it leaves an impression*

—Proust

think what you can almost see   as the surface holds
in the absences   the imprint of a brush
the ways in which the work is formed   through pressing
how one mark suggests another   the paint dries
and changes with the light   on the stretched canvas
shapes appear permanent   but the spirit lies hidden
in the scars and stains we leave   not even an echo and so
with the urge to find a point   to heighten things somehow
and make a sense beyond ourselves   we look to the uncertain place

Life Drawing

She disrobes. This moment contains the silence of fallen snow.
Her skin has something of the light from the walls and the high
studio window. Flesh glows, but not like dancing air or the moon.

Moon has a cool-flat gaze. And, dust in sunlight looks like
filaments. A body has its own blond heat. Curve on curve,
a sweeping grove. Or, like Neruda and his socks—to raise earth

to heaven. I watch her, one round hip pinked by the three-bar
heater. A landscape of dunes. I shuffle to find my place. Like an
actor finding a mark. Like a matador. Like Velásquez looking at

the Infanta Margaret Theresa, supreme with his long brushes. The
point of sight, a needle dropped. Perspective, arbitrary—a
conjuror's trick. Size of bones scratched in with a brush-end

dipped in ash. Lines scraped down to give breadth, pushed across
for depth. Muscles mapped, the bulk of form piled and squeezed
like coiled hair. An hour to find the color in another's light.

Shadows filled with burnt terra verde. Skin hatched with orange
and blue pastel, stubbed thin with rag. Vision shifts as it observes.
Light sways and sings, delinquent; changeable and faithless as the

sea. I fret to shape the dissonance of line, the melody enclosed. I
am not truthful. My pen flies to other bodies. I graze, falling back
to old marks like hoof prints. Then, as the model rises from the

dais a strand somewhere of hair or light—something sets. To see,
unlocked. How skin resembles skin. A kind of intimacy, unfamiliar
and mute. The sum of destructions becoming whole, like music.

Ode to Looking into Shadows on Market Day

The glare that stains
the chapel walls
and gossip's bench,
is not my light.
The Mayor's piped ballads
that croon,
and drown the songs
of summer birds in trees
and cages are too bright.
I like the splutter
of the dark grills
pushing wood smoke
through the cut flowers,
fresh up from the valley
this morning.
Under the eaves,
away from the stall holders
and swinging children,
looking for the shadows.
All the possibilities of shade.
To see the soft light
splitting like the silver grains
of an old photograph.
On the cobbles
of the market square,
zebra husks
of sunflower seeds,
blown into corners.
I look,
and tell the hours
by the turning hands
of the shadows.
Shadow on shadow.

On Sending Ted Kooser *Unquiet Landscape*

Winter finches jab at the bare maple.
Our copper feeder is kept empty,
we have mice in the yard.
In the wet cold a pair of birds work
the branches, searching
for insects and early buds
For a moment, the cage of end-twigs
blooms red and yellow as they squabble.
When we bought the house
there were CDs hanging
from the branches: *to scare the birds,*
the lady said. Off to Cornwall to join
her magistrate lover. Our children come out
to feel the washing frozen on the line:
a T-shirt, stiff as an axe; socks like boomerangs.
My bike has weeds in the wheels.
I sent Ted Kooser a book in a torn
Amazon sleeve. All the way to Nebraska.
I picture the tin mailbox on his
acreage; hard snow pushed high
away from the roads.
Looking for a poem for my pupils,
I found his work a week ago
and settled to it like a sparrow
in a dust bath on a summer's day.

Unquiet Landscape: Places and Ideas in 20th-Century British Painting (1991) by
Christopher Neve

Magpies

You do not have to
climb the sycamore
bending the thin branches
to see the shopping bag
beaked and twined
into the dark nest.

Just think of the rainwater,
held and pooled,
that chilled the turquoise eggs;
and of the magpies
with their cackles,
never born.

Imagine

Imagine you were the last person on Earth
and all the lost plants and animals were back, and evolving
the planet happily revolving
with certainty and worth

And then some God or other
offers you the chance to bring back humans
all the eight billions
your sister and your brother

Would you do it?
Start things up again
all the joy and all the pain
or just stay quiet

Ode to My Black Chelsea Boots

After Neruda

This same pair
of handsome boots,
having walked
with me
and fit well
these years.
All skirmish
and flirt,
we kicked
the stones
and cobbles
on the way
to other things.
Each shoe
weathered differently,
creases more
elegant than mine.
Uppers glowing
from cordovan
and turpentine;
the black of stone
and time.
Leather
taken from
some beast
has helped me
walk sometimes
graceful,
and make a delicate
noise.
My two
sleek and shining
crows.
Quiet for now.

Rotator Cuff

The movement of the big men
is delicate and precise.
Nothing is lifted
or pulled absently.
They are careful, pernickety.
Exquisite.
Here, bodies are like cars
or aircraft.
I watch their etiquette
as they carousel the free weights.
I choose the bench press machine,
shiny as a tractor.
The barbell is caged
between two steel tracks,
the movement prescribed
to an immutable vertical.
As I lower the weight
a lazy misalignment
plays metal against flesh:
gravity and simple force
(mass x *acceleration)*
tear my tendon over
and away from the bone,
elastic and tectonic.
The dropped bar slides
smoothly down the rails.
My pain is tenor, round and sharp.
No one notices.
In the changing room, I press
an ice pack to my ruined chest
as the big men, skittish and superstitious,
talk of how to get cut for competitions
with green tea and asparagus.

The Piano Tuner

Tapping keys,
turning pins for temperament.
Alone and alone.

The mutes placed to shape silence and set
a single string to sound, and then against
another. Wires squeezed and stretched to find

harmony in difference. No sooner fixed
the strings shift again in air and time,
and the music played.

Ode to the Colors on the Sea at High Tide

You must be a chaos, to give birth to a dancing star
—Nietzsche

Sandflies
coming up,
delicate as fishnet.
The water stands
fig-green in the hollows.
Clouds bunch
and thicken. The sea
turns the blue-black
of Seurat's dog.
Bending low
to skim stones
we watch colors breaking
on the swell,
like mackerel skin.
Turquoises in the shallows,
greens and blue-violet
in the troughs.
Crimson points
crest; and the dull orange
of seaweed floating
in the water.
In the white foam
the light plays. We blink
to see the changes
and mouth words
into the wind; laughing
in the hard face of the sea.
The waves drop
and edge.

In the broken
water we have all
the constellations
of the heavens
to ourselves.

L-O-V-E

Upper Mall, River Thames

In my boathouse flat
ugly as a railway carriage
we looked out through the three windows,

each as big as a man.
An eel fought with a cormorant;
wrapping itself around the bird's greasy neck.

Winded and waterlogged,
the cormorant let go
slouching up on to a buoy

to hang its wings out
to dry, like an apology;
its dragon-eyes fierce

with adrenalin. We didn't fight
or pull apart. When you left,
I ran the two bridges

between Hammersmith and Kew,
making bets with myself along the way:
If I reach the jetty before the rowers

then she will love me.
All summer, spelling love out with each stride -
L-O-V-E, like Al Green.

On the towpath, overtaking nannies
in activewear, mobiles squeezed
between shoulder and chin

like violinists; they, hurrying
to win a playground bench.
I thought of you.

Man Walks into a Bar

I sit straight-backed and tired
like a dancer or a soldier,
my hands spread

on the zinc top. I count
my fingers, lifting each one
in turn. Sun-brown hands, strong

enough to hold a child, palms striped
with spilled coffee and phenols.
I am a certificate, stamped and marked

by pimpled hospital chairs
and sleep scavenged
on hard corners. And by a birth.

I hold to the bar's tenor wobble
of laughter and intimacy;
the slide of wine glasses,

and the scrape of chairs moved
to close space. An instant shift,
I click into fatherhood.

Freddie makes a cocktail
to celebrate the Autumn baby,
the French mother; the exotic moment.

25ml pear puree
20ml lemon juice
1 B/Spoon vanilla sugar
50ml Calvados

It is newly made,
a mixture sweet and sharp.
I raise the delicate glass, and drink.

We Need to Find a Forest

In a moment, I see the world through my son's eyes.
Following ants on the pavement,
crouched and earnest, he says:
They won't ever know we are here.
Touching the low wall, he looks up
realizing something of the world.
And, in the dry, flinty air of morning,
I think that never again
will I run through the forest with the light failing
uncertain of the ground but sure I will not fall,
but that he might.

Enough

Today, we give our daughter some pencils.
She sits at a low table
on a small armchair, so that her feet lie flat
on the wooden floor. She tells us,
I am drawing a family.
She is certain of things.
She knows to turn the pencil
to keep a sharp edge. She fills each figure
with a rainbow.
Her hair falls over her eyes.
She sings the story of the picture
to herself.
She does not look up at us
until she has finished.

Today, our son rides a bike
which is Spiderman red.
We move the saddle so that his toes rest
flat on the floor. He tells us;
at school they said, just my toes
should touch, not the flat of my foot.
When he rides the bike on the road
he is certain of things. He knows
to keep to the side, even though the white lines
in the middle of the road look like a path
drawn on a map. Riding in front,
he does not turn his head when he tells us
to stop, and points to a shadow
shaped like an eagle's beak.

Today, our daughter says: *Alexa, play*
Beautiful Boy. She holds my hands
and shows me how my feet should move.
My son dances barefoot.
When we look at our children we see
ourselves. They watch how we say I
love you. They say, *I love you,*
They are certain of our love. Our children eat
space and time. They take us
by the hand and show us the right way
to catch a ball or peel an orange,
or dance. We ask them, *Why*
are you smiling? They turn and show us
how things are enough.

My Daughter Gets Dressed Listening to *Happy*

This is my favorite skirt.
I have to wear it today
because tomorrow
it won't fit.
She dresses herself.
Doesn't want pigtails.
Her necklaces and bracelets are laid out in lines
on a mammoth's tooth she found on the beach.
She aims soap bubbles across the room;
tips the bottle so the wand catches the mixture.
Each perfect round, a drop of water and glycerin
blown out and shining with rainbows.
The most brilliant things are composed of bits of color:
flower petal,
butterfly wing,
jay feather,
fish scales.
She sings *clap along,*
like the words are butterflies.
Her hem flares as she spins,
slowly dancing the labyrinth of growing up.

Wrestling Cholitas

I stand behind my mother. She presses the pedal
and feeds the cloth, threading the levers
as the needle drops. She is an eagle in the ring.

Shouts to the crowd, *El que no corre . . . vuela—*
That which doesn't run . . . flies. Tells me her wings
are borrowed. I ask her, *What bird am I?*

Her layered skirts are mint and lemon; she wears
an orange shawl, embroidered with flowers. Says,
You will be pretty, take care. Plaits my hair.

I learn from my mother how I should fight. Her shining
braids are heavy as sugar. *Our hair is our glory and our*
history. She takes me with her, every Sunday, Buys me

a soda; I make it last two hours. In the ring, she cries out,
Lucho por el amor de mi padre—I fight for the love
of my father. Lets me move the wheel slowly as she turns

the cloth. Tells me, *You are a kingfisher.* When I grow up
my pollera will be orange, cyan and blue. I lie in bed
and watch. Up and down the needle goes as she runs a seam.

Inspired by the Cholitas of Bolivia and the photographs of Todd Antony

Part 2

The great importance that Confucius placed upon the Book of Poems may be gathered from the following anecdote: one day his son Le was passing hurriedly through the Court, when he met his father standing alone lost in thought. Confucius, on seeing his son, addressed him thus "Have you read the Odes?" He replied, "Not yet." "Then," said Confucius, "if you do not learn the Odes, you will not be fit to converse with."

—Shi-King, *The Books of Odes: Introduction,*
    edited by L. Cranmer-Byng

Ode to Jean-Michel Basquiat in Which Certain Things Are Crossed Out

Some company recently was interested in buying my "aura."
—Andy Warhol

Scratching on these walls
Be a little brave
Be selfish
Be the romance of the Wild West

~~FAMOUS~~
BE FAMOUS

Bury the paint beneath your words

~~Scratch out and erase~~
~~but never so much~~
~~that they don't know~~
~~what was there~~

New York buildings are very high
Stand at the top and
drop
through
the
floors
with something like a beautiful shriek

I WILL RAISE MY VOICE I WILL STAND UP AND I WILL
LOOK YOU IN THE EYE

POISON
THIS IS NOT IN PRAISE OF ~~POISON~~

If you love her draw a ring around her finger
~~In thy orisons be all my sins rememb'red~~
Prisons Horizons
This day is too light
Somebody ~~SHUT~~ the door

Some Form of Blocking

Iggy Pop in his clapboard bungalow
in Little Haiti, Miami,
talking about his paintings.
to Sky Arts.

On his sofa
a pregnant woman
carved in foam.

He works on a canvas
which might show a face;
adding a stroke of acrylic,
he steps away
and smiles to the camera—
nothing is slyly transposed.

Filmed at a gallery show,
he seems hurt
that his paintings are
bought as souvenirs.

Another time,
talking with Stefan Brüggemann,
he says:
You block the areas,
and then you allow the rest to happen.

A Scientific Search for the Face of Elvis

Playing Marco Polo in the pool,
the crickets clicking in the old tree.
His daughter chalks numbers on
the patio, dripping water
on the squares.
Pages of a dropped book
curl up stiff as they dry.
Sprinklers stop
and a robin flies down
to lay its head on the damp lawn.
The wind comes up.

> *I used to walk in the garden*
> *with my father.*
> *He was far from things then*
> *and we had money, I suppose.*
> *He sang as he carried me,*
> *and we cried together*
> *for the sadness of the song.*

From the plane, he sees the hotel gardens
as green lozenges spilled in the desert.
They take a double suite at The Sahara.
By the pool, the towels
rolled neatly in the hopper look like
possums playing dead.
He says, *my arm is a handle*
for somebody else to pull.

> A storm comes one night.
> She sneaks up to the attic.
> The yellow bulb lights a long line
> of his mother's clothes,
> all neatly racked.

I tried on a couple of coats,
it was like she was embracing me.

The air was wrong.
The sky was wrong.
In August when the crickets
come up. Pale yellow light,
and everything washed out
in a thin haze, like it gets
in Memphis on a hot day.
The day he got called out
by the wind or the sun,
like we all do.

Three Scenes from the Making of a Revisionist Western

He drinks alone. Says,
The world isn't a bad place,
it's just big. Working on the script,
he sits on the hotel bed throwing
playing cards at his reflection.
Writes in the margin: *We all run*
out of time in the end.

A Presbyterian town thrown
together with raw lumber.
It takes three weeks to build.
The unfinished front of a cotton mill
stands blond against
the iron-dark mountain.
Cattle lift their heads
at the sound of the horses
ridden hard down gullies
and off through a river.
One night, the snow falls
so heavily it is like church music.

In the restaurant,
there are fresh flowers
on the pianola. The actor draws
white and opens with his queen's
pawn. Still wearing his duster,
he eats cowboy food
as he moves the pieces.
Corn. Beans. Succotash. Coffee.
I don't think. Usually, I don't think;
I hold it all in and then act.
In the final frame, he stands there
one arm holding the other—
like a lost child.

Bomb

alarms fused across the city like a call to prayer
people running   no one screams
necklaces of broken things on the street
i ask a young man if he will walk with me
barefoot we start looking   covered in dust
i pull my shirt over my face to breathe
all skin and no bones like the shell of things
standing still i become a mirror
the children playing in the twisted wire
men and women with white camellias worn in hope
on a branch the hanging overalls like marionettes
a husband and wife cut firewood in a car park
the city feels too big
there are no old things anymore
it takes months for the glass to leave my body

The Guardian newspaper runs a weekly feature where photographers tell the story behind their best shot. Some of the shots are from war zones and disasters. This poem is inspired by some of the testimonies which accompany the photographs.

Golden Girl

She wears a gilt dress from the clothing bank.
It shines like a coin in the sun.
The hem ripples in a breeze squeezed up from Ladbroke Grove
  Station.
She traps the silk with her knees, giggling at its life beyond her.
Above her, the barreled belly of the underpass is like the ceiling of
  a ballroom.
She walks towards the vacant units strung out beneath the buzz of
  the Westway.
Forcing herself up tight against the cold metal of the cages she
  snaps the neck of the vial.
Pressing the broken end to her nose she sniffs up.
She lies still for a while, black cobwebs and litter hang off the thin
  dress.
Sitting up, her face is loose and her head bobs as she calls out.
Her voice and her body are thick with it.
She moves across the precinct to Portobello Green, legs heavy and
  low.
Yellow poppies nod in the verge as she sits boneless on the grass.
Coming down, she checks herself like a soldier after an
  engagement.
She knows there is no secret.

How to Make a Scarecrow

Though it has no thought of keeping watch, it's not for naught that the scarecrow stands in the grain field.
—Eihei Dōgen (1200–1253)

Across the meadow
through the torn wheat. I pass the scarecrow
strung up, one busted arm waving empty.
Flies spin in the ragged shadows.

branches and fence posts

From behind the dead oak I see a man,
or the shape of a man with arms out and stiff, like a cross
or feeding birds. His wet mouth shines.
My feet hold tight in the plough-ruts.

cable ties, thin wire, duct-tape

Trapped inside a game of catch, I am stolen out of the world.
Hope rests small as a nut in my hand. Fingers pinched and stiff.
Numb-cold on the warm evening. Tethered by the snare of the
fowler.

plastic bags, shredded paper, stuffed hessian sacks

Dandelions glow in the dusk. I turn to fill myself with their yellow.
A whole field, not enough for what I need.

a worn-out fleece, a football for a head

How to leave the world: do I become the black heart of the moon,
or seep into the hollows of the night? Scratched skin. Throated.
World, cover me with feathers. Wings down, beak clamped
curious.

a hammer, nails

48

Tinnitus

I lived by a river with tides unresolved
Under the house a sewer under a wooden board it ran
Sometimes a tapping sometimes a hum in the night like a motor
I lived a time in the basement I lost the sense of what sounded
And to which sign I should be such as lover or hermit or boatman
I didn't want to keep the things that happen
Like stacking things together like money on a table
I wanted things to leak away I really did
One window light one window dark the same things over
The emotions which are easily found collected on me
Like they say I would hide by not letting things run this way or that
Nothing got better which did not float away on the river's rise
The water changes you
It was strange how I went into things
And thought everything was: I want more of this

Some Days I Wake to the Sound of Houses Moving

townhouses with spines erect
terraces slouched like drinkers at the bar
an end-of-row bowed and bent as an old nun
solitary and full
sprung ribs and hard edges
layers of change and longevity
confident improvers move in
like house martins spitting mud
skips perched on the kerb
scaffolders singing out the estuary
a hammer pushed through a plaster wall
a broken ceiling leaks out horsehair and candle wax
dusty laths fractured like animal bones
behind the boarded fireplace
a pair of workmen's leggings black with soot
and a betting slip for a greyhound
that ran in fourth at Belle Vue
our hollowed homes leave traces
pushed to the front like favored children
in the shadows
under edges
time hangs
houses roll and float
our marks smudged in the small dust

From the Loft

Looking out from our bedroom in the morning;
jets on the way to Heathrow, splinters crossing
the flat blue sky. The drama of chimneys and roof tiles,

the delicate insect precision of old aerials.
Wood pigeons clattering in the top branches
and magpies machine-gunning around the eves.

Lines of cars parked in gentle perspective,
round and ridged as ammonites. On Thursdays
the street fills for a few minutes, in reverence.

People come out and stand, small children held.
The old lady enters the street from the park,
a planned and queenly procession. Unasked

but welcomed, she blows a cracked whistle
as a young girl marches behind, arms stretched wide,
in a painted cardboard plane made from *Amazon* boxes.

Part 3

Leucon, no one's allowed to know his fate,
Not you, not me: don't ask, don't hunt for answers
In tea leaves or palms. Be patient with whatever comes.
This could be our last winter, it could be many
More, pounding the Tuscan Sea on these rocks:
Do what you must, be wise, cut your vines
And forget about hope. Time goes running, even
As we talk. Take the present, the future's no one's affair.

—Horace, *The Odes and Epodes: Book I, Ode XI,*
   translated by Burton Raffel

Ode to White

Safflower white, nudged
with a little medium
and made softer:
the yellowing can be reversed
by placing the painting
in a sunny room.
Malevich white;
a white square floats
untethered in a white field.
Flake Lead white scraped
off coiled metal strips
stewed in clay pots
with vinegar and cow dung:
bright like milk.

Goya and Vermeer,
pale and choleric;
dying from the white
sucking the sweet lead
from their brush-tips—
teeth edged with blue.

Memory comes white
in flecks; like dust, like sand,
like spilled flour.
The white-drenched road,
the luminous hospital.
A private room with dazzling walls,
white bed sheets shadowed grey
with the pressed marks of the iron.
A low table with a Gideon Bible,
flared light comes up off the water glass.
As I wait, I weave two loose white threads
from the blanket; one turns violet in contrast.

White shroud.
White ashes.
White bones.
White moon, silver-white.
White water over shattered rock.

My daughter in a print dress
counting the blossoms on the sand cherry
trailing low over the dunes is two times white,
maybe three. She starts over
every time she reaches ten.

Acclimatizing by the Snout of the Barum Glacier

Camped out on a grassy shelf waiting for our blood
to build; we measure the day by the turning shadows.
The Chinese test their guns across the divide; each report

stretched out, sad as whale-song. Sun lights the ridge orange
as it falls. Violet mountains turn iron black as the day goes out,
and the wind comes down cold. Watching for meteor trails

as the constellations shift, we eat canned cheese and sardines
on flat breads from the fire. The long night moves over us.
Tents glow green and yellow; and then dark. In the deep night,

the zigzag of a torch pulling someone to the latrine.
Animal eyes flash platinum in the battery light—a toad
come up from the deep grass. The night sounds

are small here. In the unbroken black the terrible clarity
of things left undone: people not cared enough
about to keep; the futile vanity of ascent.

The Garden

When she asked me
what I meant by love,
I thought to fill my hands
with all the beautiful plants;
having things in rows
and cropped; and up.
Instead, I sat down
in the deep green
like a cat or fallen
fruit. Laid out
in the flowerbed,
one leg bent
and my shirt all out.
A bird came down.
I filled my hands with soil
and closed my fists.
I thought of flying angels,
as the delicate flies rose up.
At that time, I lived my life
in big stitches
and jagged cuts
on straight roads.
Not looking what was in
the folds or the rising dust
I sought only the touch
needed for things
to be solid. But
in the small garden
I felt the air
that lights things,
and the tissue
of colors.
When she asked me
what I mean by love.

The Enormous Matter of Landscape

I live alone everywhere
—Walter Tevis, *The Man Who Fell to Earth*

The hills change color
in the autumn; water flares
red and orange as the wind

pushes hard on the lake.
The birds are leaving; away,
like an armada or smoke

from the chimney. I am drunk
in the afternoon sun.
Brightness falls from the air.

It comes down and goes out
on the water, takes me with it
to the far edges. Sitting on a bare log

to drink warm gin from a flask,
the chill air is on my arms. I have
the quiet lake with old reeds

up like wire; the sense of water,
and the clickings of insects.
I cannot say this is my place.

Reflections on a Clear Night

Life is a solitary cell whose walls are mirrors
　　　　　　　　—Eugene O'Neill

I stop at the water's edge
and look in
to see like music
an image better
than the real me
and the moon in the lake
bouncing and wobbling
becoming still again
as I drink in the illusion
and accept its truth

to throw a stone into my reflection
expecting the world above to also move
the ripples that spread and fade
clearer somehow
everything with sharper colors
passing upside down
in the water
a doubled mirror
of light on light
this is all that I will ever be

Walking Up Steep Hill to School on a Snowy Morning

Laughing as we fall/we hang
to the walls/like drunks//
Winced feet/in wet shoes//
Crying out/an elbow hits the cobbles/
a knee bounces off/a door jamb//
An old couple shuffle past/dressed
tightly for the cold//
Sturdy and trim/
bending over their feet//
The man with his right hand
light on the iron rail/
the woman her left//
Flat-footed and small-stepped/
we copy them/all the way up
to the cathedral school//
A single line/in respectful/
penguin waddle//
The husband and wife smiling
to have children again//

Autumn, You Are No Friend of Mine

It is too early
for the itchy click of the boiler;
the rising sourness of old dust
cooking up behind the radiators.

You are a clammy thing, all ooze,
tree resins seeping out; floored fruit
blackened and furred, alive and dancing
with beetles and wasps.

Not for you the elegant tilt
of a disreputable cocktail by the pool;
yours is a farmyard cider from a clay cup,
stinking of the muckheap.

Be reasonable, and wait;
you can have your yellow leaves and thistledown,
and the sheaves and mellow fruits,
but don't take the long day back behind the Earth.

I will not button my hasty shirt
against the morning mist that hangs
like damp cloth. I am outside, sockless
eating figs warm as a cat's belly.

So, I won't care for your plenty;
your felted berries and swelling fruits.
For I loved and had love in summer,
gone now with the last leaf.

Falling Down

I fly beyond my shadow;
sun-struck they say,
when madness comes.

Up here wind cuts, cold
even in the blasting light;
I am not a dazzling eagle.

I am a cracked leaf,
brittle and blown;
pushed around.

It aches to be here,
fierce and unsteady.
I do not have myself.

So I fall, sharp
as a splinter
from a lathe;

and cut
the water,
to feel solid.

Funeral Song

I hold a piece
of fallen headstone.

Rubbing the dirt away
I see letters

but not the words
that marked a life.

The trace of the chisel
is still sharp in the stone;

the surface smoothed
and finished

by a hand made hard
from working.

I drop the rock.
There is enough here, I say.

Of the Styles of Handwriting, and the Direction of the Lines Written

A natural unstudied hand, then, is the only true test of character.
—Henry Frith

(1) If it be even

Straightforward and firm, my
letters stand like soldiers of the
steel frame of the classroom's
cold window; keeping to the
lines I will walk in health and
be a rock and never look to be
this way or that; or be the one.

(2) If it be ascending

I am
the reaching
hand, scrambled
to for my ardor; lines
sloping up, ambitious to
spin away; wanting of form
and harmony, but firm and sure—
I will be called lucky, and be careless.

(3) The descending writing

Drooping downwards, with sad fingers
I will never pry or seek but stay home,
ungloved and grey-faced;
even if poked and bored,
and smothered I will
always yield and
give up to the
imagined
fear.

(4) Unevenly made

Mine is formed by struggle: straight
to rise only to fall away,
unfirm; too fast to start
and then winded;
dragged down
by worry or bad luck;
summoned untimely
and hopeful early, prodigious—
I will be scorched and spotted
like a new leaf
in the frost.

Butterfly Guilt

Her careful father
pierced them with pins,
killing each one for a picture.
She went hunting with him
and caught a beauty
in a fresh mountain meadow
with the tall-grass all around.
On feet of air
she watched it fold and open
in spectacular symmetry.
It flew from the net
in jagged spirals, nap all torn
by the muslin
and the caring hands.

Haystacks

to scent the barn and sweeten milk far into the bleaching winter
—Robert Morgan

The same soft light spread over everything.
The wild barley bends in the verge. Haystacks lined up
like widows queuing for bread. All day combing

the sheafs, the women throw a bundle of straw
and watch it turn in the air. They wear trousers
to work the fields, on the flat edge out from the hills.

The colors are earth and old grass. Villagers
dress carefully for church. Footsteps of children
make the wooden chapel creak. Here, the old people

wait for winter. She kissed him in the hollow heart
of a haystack. Her hopes stuck like splinters in her
thumb. Now the wheat grows brittle and lies down.

/ heretic /

for Carlton Pearson

The renewing,
everybody say the renewing.
Up on the mountain,
we sing as if listening
to ourselves. The song, the song,
the song, the song, come out.
Come out. Come out now.
Though your outer self be
wasting away it will be
renewed. You are the lamb
without blemish or spot.
Go down there
and cover them.
Unsaved, a baby
dying in a dirt field.
For such a time as this,
I leave the hero's ship
and all the swagger. I leave
to measure the shadows
of the Earth because
the shadow, the shadow
of my body, lies there.
It is not so hard to give up Hell,
you do not have to expect devils.
Renounce them and turn in the path,
merely turn in the path.
We are then as two stones
come together by gravity.
And between, vines will be planted
and corn will spring up.
When I leave for the sea,
I will take you with me
—far from this hilly place.

The Song of the Self

Inspired by a Sanskrit translation

We feel the Self dampened and magnified
like breaking waves, shelved and shored by wind—
but this shoaling is not the Self.
The Self lies beneath five layers,
felt through the scratch and flare of the Self,
like layered crinolines moving to the rhythm of song.

The *veil of the body* is made of food and stars.
It has architecture,
like a bucket or a cupboard.
It encloses our warmth and vigor—
but this dull shell is not the Self.

The *veil made of breath* governs inspiration, growth and speech.
From it comes hunger and thirst.
Instantly tangible and vital,
we feel it in our mouth and ribs—
but this flow of air is not the Self.

The *veil made of mind* gives us pride in possessions,
it holds our prejudices and preferences.
It is subject to shifts and changes
and uplift and denudations, like the Earth—
it is transitory, so it cannot be the Self.

The *veil of knowledge* holds reason and consciousness.
It directs us like a compass.
We use it to measure and sift
like the haul of a trawler's net—
but this weighted catch is not the Self.

The *veil of bliss* holds our happiness and pleasure.
It also carries sadness and regret.
This light and dark holds something of what it is to be,
the to and the fro—
but this play of colors is not the Self.

When the five veils unpeel, or slip and shift away together,
the Self lies revealed through the reflection of all that moves and
changes.
From the shaking of a leaf
to the massive orbits of planets and the slow revolution of the sun,
the Self reflects in all that is and will be—and shines.

About the Author

Kris Spencer is a British poet. His poems have been published in journals in the UK, Ireland, the US, Europe and SE Asia. He is an elected Fellow of the Royal Geographical Society. The RGS is a grand institution that celebrates explorers.

Kris is a teacher living and working in West London. He encourages pupils, teachers and parents to see the poetry in things. He was born and grew up in a village outside Bolton. Previously, he has studied, worked and lived in Hull, Cincinnati, Oxford, and the Bailiwick of Jersey.

Kris is married with two children.